The Evolving Language of Innovation

Jon Glasco

The Evolving Language of Innovation

A Glossary of Terms

Jon Glasco

First Edition | Revised 2018

An original publication of Glasco Clark
Associates

Cover image: © Vectoraart | Dreamstime.com -
People On-line Share Business Idea Concept
Design

ISBN-13: 978-1491051092
ISBN-10: 1491051094

First Edition Revised [R11.0]

PRINTED IN THE USA

Author's Notes:

Designations used by companies to distinguish their products are often claimed as trademarks. In all instances where the author is aware of a claim, the designated names appear in initial capital letters. However, readers should contact the appropriate companies for more information regarding trademarks and registration.

Efforts have been made to trace copyright holders, but if any have been overlooked, the author will take the necessary steps at the first opportunity.

"Knowledge has to be improved, challenged,

and increased constantly,

or it vanishes."

– Peter Drucker

CONTENTS

Photo by Riccardo Annandale on Unsplash

INTRODUCTION

Innovators communicate in a unique language that emerges from the worlds of R&D, product design, technology transfer, entrepreneurial ventures, academic research, thought leadership studies, professional media, networking, and multinational projects.

Communicating in the language of innovation helps to make our conceptual thinking and our ideas understandable and visible to others. It has an impact not only on what we think but on how we think and cooperate with others during creative activities and innovation projects.

The evolving language of innovation includes terminology from the modes of thought known as *analytical, left-brain thinking* and *intuitive, right-brain thinking*. In an innovation project, both of these modes are essential. In this glossary—with more than 150 entries—I include terms from both types of thinking.

I hope that innovators from industry, education, government, non-profits and other spheres of interest will find this glossary useful.

Jon Glasco

Glasco Clark Associates
Capture the Letter and Spirit of Enterprise™

GLOSSARY OF INNOVATION TERMS

Absorptive capacity

Ability to recognize and absorb new knowledge and emerging ideas and apply these to the challenge of innovation.

Additive comparison

A tool used for comparing alternative concepts and solutions; helpful when the ratings of multiple criteria are in different dimensions or scales.

Relies on converting the ratings to dimensionless values (which are then multiplied by a weighting factor to reach a final score for each alternative).

Adopter categories

Groups of consumers (or citizens) based on their readiness to use a new service or product. Five main categories: innovators, early adopters, early majority, late majority, laggards.

Adoption process

A chain of events that starts with consumer (or citizen) awareness of an innovation, followed by trial use, and eventually leading to acceptance, trust and regular usage.

Advocate

In an innovation ecosystem, this is a respected opinion leader who supports a new solution or concept; offers expertise to influence key stakeholders. Helps to secure approval for an innovation project.

The Evolving Language of Innovation

Adjacent innovation

Applying a technology or product strength (or other capability) to build a position in a new market. [Nagji and Tuff, 2012]

Affect display

A form of non-verbal communications—e.g., expressions or actions that signal one's emotions, whether positive or negative. May influence the flow of ideas, knowledge and information.

Alternate choice technique

A persuasive communications technique which involves suggesting two equally acceptable choices to the listener; helps to avoid a "no" option during early-stage idea generation activities.

Ansoff matrix

Market and product innovation tools (created by Igor Ansoff) used to help planners consider alternative growth options via existing and/or new products and markets.

Four possible product / market combinations help planners decide what strategy and actions to take:

- **Market penetration** – existing markets with existing products
- **Product development** – existing markets with new products
- **Market development** – new markets with existing products
- **Diversification** – new markets and new products

The Evolving Language of Innovation

Aspiration level

A specific outcome that an individual or group wants – usually based on a perception and mental model of risks, costs and benefits. For a given situation, people will have different models and therefore different aspiration levels.

In an innovation project, it is important for the facilitator to have an understanding of conflicting aspiration levels. (See: *Mental model*)

Asset-driven innovation (ADI)

A process of finding new ways to create value from existing or to-be-acquired assets. Involves the use of untapped asset value as an *entry point* for ideas.

Participants in innovation are encouraged to explore new opportunities for both *tangible assets* (R&D infrastructure, production facilities, working capital) and *intangible* (unique skills, management practices, favorable contracts, partnerships, path dependency advantages, patents, copyrights, customer databases, etc.) (See: *Entry point*)

Assumption reversal

An idea generation technique where key assumptions regarding a particular scenario are listed, and then reversed before addressing the same scenario to discover what new solutions emerge.

Attribute listing

A problem-solving technique that consists of listing all the essential attributes or characteristics of a scenario or problem and then analyzing each attribute with the goal of trying to change them in multiple ways.

Barriers to innovation

Obstacles and problems that hinder attempts to innovate. Includes technology hurdles, cost overruns, lack of knowledge, funding shortfalls, poor climate for innovation, risk-averse culture, regulatory barriers, and lack of commitment.

Brainstorming

Method for generating a large volume of ideas and concepts quickly and spontaneously in a mostly unstructured meeting; sometimes called an ideation session. Success of the method depends on having a facilitator, a good climate, and the ability to suspend judgment on the ideas produced.

Breakthrough

A concept or solution that is "new to the world" and reaches beyond anything that's been accomplished before. May involve high risk and often requires exceptional persuasive communication skill to secure approval for development. (See: *New-to-the-world solution*)

> "Discovery consists of seeing what everybody has seen and thinking what nobody has thought." Albert Szent-Györgyi de Nagyrápolt, Hungarian physiologist, Nobel prize winner, 1937

Business model

A wide range of formal and informal descriptions and analyses that represent (a) the core elements of an organization and (b) how the organization creates and captures value.

Business Model Canvas

A strategic planning template for creating new business models (or documenting current models). Usually includes the key elements of value proposition, infrastructure, customers, and finances. [Osterwalder et al, 2010].

Business model innovation

Design of a new (or disruptive) business model through reinvention of two or more elements of an existing model to create value in a new way [Lindgardt et al, 2009]

Camelot scenario

A technique to help innovation teams think beyond the status quo. Participants are asked to create an ideal solution or situation (the "Camelot") and compare this with their current situation or problem, e.g., what are the differences? Why do these exist? How should we design an ideation session to create new opportunities and solutions that bring us closer to the ideal scenario? [Higgins, 1994]

Capitalist

A capitalist is skilled in locating and securing funding and other resources needed by innovators; the commitment of the capitalist may be an assumed, non-traditional role (beyond the traditional job description).

Cause-and-effect analysis

A diagramming technique that displays in detail the possible causes of a problem and the expected benefits of a solution.

Change management

A process to enable a transition, with minimal disruption, from an existing situation to an improved situation or system. A process to enable a transition, with minimal disruption, from an existing situation to an improved situation or system.

Climate for innovation

The internal environment and attitude toward innovation and risk-taking; critical to the success of innovation projects.

Participants in such projects must believe they are encouraged to generate new ideas, think beyond existing boundaries, experiment with breakthrough concepts and at times take risks they would not consider in the normal course of their work.

Co-creation

An approach to innovation whereby multiple entities (e.g., government, citizens, companies, universities and / or non-profits) work together to share ideas and knowledge and jointly develop a service, product, solution or other mutually beneficial outcome.

Codified knowledge

Knowledge or information content that has been documented in some form of communications medium (printed document, engineering drawings, software, website content, blog, e-mail message, social and professional networks, intranet, video and audio recordings, multimedia presentations, digitized images).

Co-innovation risk

The extent to which the success of an innovation depends on the success and commercialization of partners' innovations.

Collaborative community

An innovative community organized around and motivated by a shared purpose. Diverse capabilities in the community stimulate innovation and interdependent knowledge-based cooperation. [Adler et al, 2011]

Common ground

A communications technique involving discovery of similar thinking among people that have different views on key issues. It is often the initial point for creating a dialogue for innovation and problem solving.

Concept development

An early phase of the innovation process that involves transforming ideas into realizable (and fundable) concepts; often relies on experimenting with concepts through the use of models and prototypes with the objective of identifying gaps in knowledge and making the ideas more concrete and acceptable to decision makers.

Concept map

A visual model of a system or situation; designed to increase understanding (rather than accuracy). Used as a visual tool to show how a new solution might work.

The Evolving Language of Innovation

Connection mode

A creative process of visualizing something new by connecting ideas and thoughts which were previously considered unrelated.

> "It is the tension between creativity and skepticism that has produced the stunning and unexpected findings of science." Carl Sagan, American astronomer, astrochemist and author, 1934-1995

Consensus building

A group-oriented approach to planning and decision making that seeks agreement of all or most participants and step-by-step resolution of issues and objections.

The approach aims to be inclusive, participatory and solution-driven. However, it is usually not a good approach when an innovative solution is required and may hinder development of a healthy *climate for innovation.*

A facilitator works toward building a shared paradigm of success during the consensus building process. (See: *Shared paradigm*)

> "Experimenting with many diverse—and sometimes seemingly absurd— ideas is crucial to innovation ... experiments are particularly valuable when performed early so that unfavorable options can be eliminated quickly." Stefan Thomke

Core innovation

Process of managing incremental changes in existing products or taking small steps into new markets. [Nagji and Tuff, 2012]

The Evolving Language of Innovation

Creative industries

A wide spectrum of innovative activities in advertising, architecture, art, crafts, design, fashion, film, TV, radio, music, publishing, software, computer games, toys, etc.

Decision tree

A planning tool based on a tree diagram that serves as a model of alternative decisions and helps to estimate and clarify consequences (risks, costs, profitability, utility, etc.).

Used to identify the alternatives most likely to achieve a desired objective.

Generally not used in the early stages of an innovation project, but can be helpful after concepts are selected for implementation and need to be compared prior to committing resources.

Delphi method

A highly systematic method of analysis and forecasting that relies on a group of selected experts who respond to questionnaires in multiple rounds.

Following each round, an independent facilitator delivers an anonymous summary of results and asks experts to revise their earlier replies (based on replies from other group members). The process is designed to converge on a best solution or answer.

Applied as an innovation technique when the facilitator wants each expert to think through each round without immediate reaction from others.

Derived demand

A requirement for a product, service or application created by the adoption and use of another product or innovation.

Design thinking

A solution-driven way of creative thinking; starts with a goal or vision of the innovative outcome (rather than starting with a specific problem or opportunity). Explores the parameters of possible ways to reach the solution. Relies on synthesis (rather than analysis) of ideas and concepts.

Diffusion model

A marketing tool used to show how the communication of an innovation leads to growing numbers of adopters over time (in a population of potential customers).

Direct analogy

A problem-solving approach that looks for similar situations to the current one and asks questions such as: "Where and how has this problem – or something analogous – been solved in the past? What does the prior solution offer in terms of new ideas, entry points and knowledge?" (See: *Entry point*)

Disjunctive model

A model of attitude development which stresses that the consumer (or citizen) expects a minimum level of satisfaction on the most essential attributes of a new product or service but not on every attribute.

The Evolving Language of Innovation

Diverse resource

Someone with a creative spirit; an articulate idea generator recruited from the periphery of the project or organization. Usually adds new perspective and ideas from external sources

Dominant position

An opinion or point of view by a person of authority; one who often controls the process of innovation (or may hinder the process through an unwillingness to change views or accept the ideas of others)

Ecosystem

A group of interdependent entities and their environment. Example of an *innovation ecosystem*: A pro-innovation network or cluster of suppliers, customers, business partnerships, R&D ventures, entrepreneurial firms, investors, universities, government agencies, and trade associations.

Ecosystem leader

An organization that serves a central role in enabling other members of the ecosystem to "move toward shared visions to align their investments and to find mutually supportive roles." [Moore, 1996]

Embedded knowledge

Knowledge that becomes rooted in a company's products, services, systems or processes. A specialist applies expertise to create something of value that depends on what has been learned through experience and training.

The Evolving Language of Innovation

Many business and manufacturing processes are developed from what was once the knowledge (perhaps tacit) of individual experts.

Emergent solution

An innovative solution created by a group during a process of creative thinking and problem solving. Instead of relying on first ideas presented (which may not satisfy all stakeholders), the solution emerges after participants share knowledge, perspectives and fresh ideas and discover an outcome that *integrates* the goals of all participants. (Kaner, p. 27)

Enlightened experimentation

A stage in the process of innovation when ideas or concepts are transformed into a prototype or model, enabling a systematic cycle of testing as a way to create and refine products. Often relies on technologies to reduce the marginal cost of experiments. (Thomke, p. 179)

Entry point

The selection of an issue or situation from which to generate ideas. Selection of an entry point is important in ideation sessions, because the sequence in which ideas flow may affect the conclusion and ultimate solution, even when the cluster of ideas is the essentially the same. (See: *Task headline*)

Exploratory thinking

A process of thought that avoids evaluation and decision-making in the early stages. The goal is to experiment with ideas, sometimes fail, learn from the experiment, and keep going toward other, untested ideas and concepts.

The Evolving Language of Innovation

The opposite of a decision-mode style of thinking, which is appropriate when you need to take action or reach a decision quickly.

> "If I find 10,000 ways something won't work, I haven't failed. I am not discouraged, because every wrong attempt discarded is another step forward." Thomas A. Edison, US inventor, 1847-1931

Facilitator

Someone who serves as a guide for the innovation process; plans and facilitates team meetings, ideation sessions and problem-solving activities. May also be in charge of process design. Usually is not involved in content.

This role is essential in most innovation projects. The facilitator builds and maintains a healthy climate for innovation and ensures new ideas are encouraged and nurtured.

> "If you put forward a new idea, someone will immediately tell you what is wrong with it and why it will not work – a sort of management by exception, totally misapplied. We pay an enormous price for this cultural quirk." Nolan, p.62

Fishbone diagramming

A technique to (a) identify all the possible causes of a problem or situation; and (b) conduct ideation sessions to address the main causes. Helps innovators to examine the total problem space rather than looking at a narrow cross section.

The Evolving Language of Innovation

Gatekeeper

An innovation team member who receives probing questions from outsiders and deals with negative feedback and other information that may cause disruption to the innovation project. Finds ways to manage the interruptions and minimize impact to the project. (See: *Non-traditional role)*

Groan zone

A state of mind between divergent and convergent thinking; where a group experiences frustration and discomfort with the process of innovation and / or their role in the process. [Kaner, 2007]

Headlining

Method of using a brief phrase or sentence to present an idea before giving any supporting details; helps to focus attention on the nature of the idea without getting distracted.

When the climate is less than ideal, many idea generators will have a tendency to pre-sell their idea before revealing it. This causes the listeners to focus on details, and they may not hear the idea when it is presented.

The quality and quantity of ideas increases when participants apply the headlining technique with ideas often expressed as "I wish" or "How to" statements. (See: *Synectics*)

Hidden position

A potentially innovative and valuable position or viewpoint held by a team member or functional department that lingers in the background of innovation projects; often kept in the background and not revealed to the project team due to perceived risks, fear of failure, or other barriers.

Idea champion

Someone with an entrepreneurial mindset who promotes and encourages idea generation, finds ways to nurture and develop new concepts, and advises other innovators on both the content and process for innovation management success.

Idea portfolio

A structured knowledge base of ideas, concepts, unexplored opportunities, potential solutions and other intellectual assets that promote and stimulate exploratory thinking.

Idea profile

A brief description on the nature and characteristics of an idea, its positive features, potential value, areas of concern, and proposed next steps. The idea profile serves as a tool in clarifying the idea and building momentum. (see Glasco, p. 58)

Ideation

The idea generation and brainstorming phase of an innovation project; designed to obtain a wide range and large volume of fresh ideas to address complex challenges and problems.

This is a highly creative endeavor (rather than analytical) and depends on having a good climate for innovation and an understanding of *suspended judgment.*

A process facilitator works toward the generation and nurturing of ideas and avoids evaluation of feasibility or risk. (See: *Innovation project*)

Inflection point

An observable change in the nature of customer demand (or other market trends) that signals an opportunity for innovation as a means to create competitive advantage.

The key to recognizing an inflection point often depends on being able to understand the pattern among diverse (perhaps conflicting) market signals. (See: *Weak signals*)

Information asymmetry

An issue that occurs in situations where investors consider a new opportunity, and the entrepreneur-manager knows more (or less) about the business (technologies, markets, business strengths and weaknesses). This asymmetry – when one party to an investment transaction knows more than other stakeholders – increases the risk of miscommunication and conflict.

In / out listening

The mind wanders! It's not a bad thing, but most of us, when listening to someone else, will tune out occasionally. This happens because of the volume and diversity of information, pressures and priorities on the mind in a typical day.

The Synectics method of innovation teaches that in/out listening is beneficial when you recognize that it's happening. When you resume listening, it is often because a new idea has emerged in the mind, perhaps one that connects with something the speaker said earlier.

The key is to write a quick note or reminder phrase on the idea before it is obscured by other information.

Innovation

The process of creative thinking and development of new ideas and concepts, combined with opportunity assessment and implementation.

> "Innovation is what happens when new thinking is successfully introduced in and valued by organizations." Dodgson, p. 12

Innovation audit

A structured process of reviewing a completed project or process to identify what worked, what problems occurred, and generate ideas and recommendations for the future.

Innovation district

A location in a city which undergoes urban regeneration for the purpose of creating a high-tech zone and innovation ecosystem to support startup firms, entrepreneurs, business incubators, knowledge sharing and spillover effects. (Katz and Wagner, 2014)

Innovation hub

A specialized node in a network or ecosystem of innovators that connects to many other nodes and serves as a collaborative and creative resource.

The Evolving Language of Innovation

Innovation management

The process, tools, climate and resources needed to generate, nurture and develop new ideas, concepts and solutions – and to derive value from the results.

Innovation management process

The interconnected steps taken to achieve innovation; often designed and re-designed while a project is in motion. Success of the process often depends on non-traditional roles and the ability to maintain a favorable climate for innovation.

Innovation project

An assembly of resources, activities, knowledge sharing and ideas created to design and build something new. Most innovation projects are less confined than traditional, structured projects, and are usually characterized by high energy levels.

Instant version

A technique that enables a facilitator to gather initial thoughts of experts on how to solve a complex problem or create a breakthrough product. Participants are asked to provide a summary or sketch of their ideas on what the ultimate solution or design might look like, after making assumptions about removal of barriers (e.g. technology barriers, lack of financing, regulatory constraints, etc).

The technique may be used in small groups or one-on-one interviews. The goal is to capture free-flowing visionary thoughts and ideas which may have been obscured by barriers to change, perceived risk or a past situation.

The Evolving Language of Innovation

Intellectual asset management (IAM)

The process of creating, identifying, leveraging, managing and applying intellectual assets in ways that maximize value; involves management of both tacit and codified knowledge.

IAM is related to innovation management through the new opportunities that an enterprise pursues to capture the value of its intellectual assets. (See: *ADI*)

Intent versus effect

Sometimes what you intend to communicate is not what the listener hears. In an innovation project, many new ideas and terms emerge, making it difficult for team members to communicate. When someone offers a new idea, the listener(s) may not understand the intent.

This is why it's important to use the *paraphrasing* technique as a means to communicate to the idea generator that you are making an attempt to understand the idea and the intent. (See: *Paraphrasing*)

> "The mismatch between intent and effect is a common cause of communication failure." Nolan, p.19

Intrapreneur

A creative employee in an established organization who has many of the characteristics of an entrepreneur. Takes responsibility for innovating and turning ideas into new products and solutions.

The Evolving Language of Innovation

Invention

A new device, method or process developed from study and experimentation (*The American Heritage Dictionary, 4th Edition*)

Inverse brainstorming

A form of idea generation that starts from the opposite side of traditional brainstorming. With the inverse method, a project team is given a new solution and asked to look for potential problems in design, implementation, testing and marketplace acceptance.

Issue identification

One of the initial phases in an innovation project; when the goal is to identify problems, opportunities, threats, emerging situations or other drivers of innovation.

It isn't necessary to define issues in precise terms in this phase, but rather to compress the issue into the form of actionable "How to" or "I wish" statements – which encourage the generation of fresh ideas in the *Ideation* phase. (See: *Springboards and Task headlines*)

Itemized response

An idea-nurturing technique which calls upon a group to look first for the positive aspects of an idea and then convert its drawbacks into "how to" statements.

The how-to's are used to invite further development of the idea and find ways to increase its acceptability. (See: *Synectics*)

The Evolving Language of Innovation

Kepner-Tregoe

A systematic process used to maximize the skills and knowledge of subject matter experts when addressing a specific problem, opportunity or decision. Also known as the "rational process", it usually consists of several parts:

- Situation appraisal
- Problem analysis
- Decision analysis
- Opportunity assessment

Knowledge investment

The use of money and other resources to develop or acquire knowledge; an ingredient of innovation management. May include investing in various combinations of:

- Technology transfer
- University collaboration
- Content management and digitization
- Knowledge management and knowledge-sharing initiatives
- Research and development
- Market and competitive research
- Thought leadership programs
- Mergers and acquisitions

Knowledge-sharing network

Formal and informal interaction that enables groups, project teams and ecosystems to share knowledge and ideas, collaborate on creative tasks, and overcome barriers to innovation.

Knowledge turn

The time required for an idea or experiment to proceed from initial hypothesis to results in the marketplace (Grove, 1998)

The Evolving Language of Innovation

Lateral thinking

A form of thinking and reasoning about a problem or challenge in a manner that is not obvious or consistent with current perceptions; a method of thinking concerned with changing perceptions and mental models; generating ideas and solutions that are not within reach through traditional logic or analysis.

The term lateral thinking was originally created by Edward de Bono. (See: *Vertical thinking*)

> "In lateral thinking one does not mind being wrong on the way to a solution ... it may be necessary to go through a wrong idea in order to get to a position from which the correct path is visible." De Bono, p. 232

Leap-ahead thoughts

The mental phenomenon of listening and interpreting at a rate that exceeds the speaker's rate of communicating – often leading to a perceived conclusion that may not match the speaker's intent. (See: *Intent versus effect*)

Leapfrog

In idea generation, this is a logic-defying thought that enables innovators to mentally leap over assumptions or barriers which block the emergence of new ideas.

Market framing

A process that combines scenario planning with creativity and innovation tools. The technique helps planners find new ways to explore possible outcomes in an unstable, developing market and generate ideas on how to prepare for the likely scenario. (See: *Scenario planning)*

Marketing innovation

New methods and improvements relating to the functions of pricing, marketing communications, promotion, distribution, packaging, and thought leadership.

Market stretch

Using innovation tools to develop new ideas for extending the life of a product or service.

Enables planners to generate proactive ideas to deal with an expected sales decline or loss in market share. Usually relies on entry points such as new packaging, new product uses, product enhancements, and changes in promotion and sales channels. (See: *Entry point*)

Mashup

Intuitive and creative blending of dissimilar concepts or ideas. Can be applied at various levels of innovation, e.g., product design, complex systems, business model, national and regional innovation strategies, etc.

Megacommunity

A sphere of cooperation where businesses, government and civil society share knowledge and work together (without compromising individual values) to deliver results that benefit society. (See: *Social innovation*)

Mental model

An individual viewpoint on how things work in an industry, market, organization or functional area. May be difficult to quantify or communicate to others. May hinder the process of innovation due to beliefs that *assumed barriers* cannot be overcome.

The role of a facilitator is to guide innovation team members by bringing mental models into focus so that barriers can be visualized, discussed in a constructive manner, and ideas generated for positive action.

Metaphor

A figurative use of language in which two different modes of thought or ideas are linked by some similarity. The metaphor treats one thing as though it were something else so that a resemblance or characteristic that would usually not be in view is highlighted. (See: *Direct Analogy*)

Through an *extended metaphor*, innovators are motivated to develop a new (primary) line of thought with multiple (subsidiary) ideas for further development.

> "Key metaphors help determine what and how we perceive and how we think about our perceptions." Meyer H. Abrams

Mind map

A diagramming technique that displays words, ideas, tasks, or other items linked in a radial structure around a key word or idea. Image-centric diagrams are used to represent semantic or other connections between pieces of information.

The Evolving Language of Innovation

Used to generate, visualize, structure, and classify ideas, and help in organization, problem solving, and scenario planning.

Mini-dominate options

An approach to strategy when a company has limited resources and is unable to build a dominant market position.

The mini-dominate method encourages people to explore new ideas for concentrating their marketing efforts on selected market segments or geographic regions; sometimes combined with ideation sessions that focus on how to conserve and focus resources on the most attractive opportunities.

Minimalist outlook

A group or individual perspective that promotes simplicity in design. In an innovation project, the minimalist is someone with creative skills who is effective in seeing through the complexities of a situation and generating ideas for highly simple solutions, strategies, product designs, etc.

Minimax principle

A theory about decision-making that suggests individuals seek to maximize rewards and minimize costs.

In zero-sum game theory and statistics, the principle is thought of as minimizing the maximum possible loss. Alternatively, it can be applied to maximizing the minimum gain (maximin). Applications include complex gaming situations and decision-making under uncertainty.

Useful in the late stages of an innovation project to create a dialog for discussion of uncertainties.

Morphology analysis

A problem-solving method that enables the generation of many ideas in a brief time span. The method relies on development of a detailed matrix with specific characteristics, adjectives and words related to the problem. The goal of the analysis is to force a set of characteristics against another to create fresh ideas and new insights.

Network architect

Someone who maintains awareness of key contacts and resources in adjacent networks of interest to an innovation project. Assists the project team in obtaining and absorbing knowledge and ideas from other networks.

Skilled at exploring new networks for relevant information and building information-sharing relationships and boundary-spanning linkages.

New-to-the-world solution

A completely new approach to a problem or opportunity; usually difficult to articulate or define in early stages; may depend on several innovations and inventions working in harmony. Typically a complex and high-risk endeavor.

Niche fusion

A strategy for deploying a new technology by dominating multiple niche positions in a market. Success depends on overcoming a technology barrier, introducing an innovative product or service, and fusing together two or more niches to build a competitive advantage in the larger niche.

> A niche fusion strategy "is suitable for technologies with a rate of performance improvement that is steep relative to alternatives." – MacMillan and McGrath, p. 165

Non-traditional role

A function that someone performs which is outside their traditional job description or assigned role. On some types of innovation projects, a non-traditional role may not be officially sanctioned or defined, but is one recognized as essential to success of the project.

May involve some degree of career development risk to the person assuming the role (but it is part of the project leader's role to ensure personal risks are minimized).

Nordic model

An innovative model of sustainable economic growth. Key features of the model include the collective interaction of globalization and risk sharing throughout society; a market-friendly attitude toward international trade; investment in human capital; and widespread trust in the welfare state.

Offer

One of the five basic forms of innovation dialogue, as suggested by Synectics theory. An 'offer' is an idea, suggestion or other communication intended to be helpful.

The Evolving Language of Innovation

The other forms of innovation dialogue are:

- **Accept** – "I like your idea."
- **Reject** – "It doesn't fit with our strategy, it's too risky."
- **Build** – "I like this idea, and here's another thought that adds to what you're suggesting."
- **Question** – Any probing communication (often placing the idea generator on the defensive).

Open innovation

A concept and theory that promotes sharing of research, knowledge and innovation with external entities, including partners, competitors, customers and other stakeholders. [Chesbrough, 2003]

Open-ended problem solving

A group method of innovation to discover solutions for a complex problem with multiple dimensions. Each member of the group presents a perspective or concern about a troublesome aspect or dimension of the problem, and a facilitator leads the group through an idea generation session. To maintain momentum, the facilitator encourages the group to make assumptions about barriers, gaps in knowledge, funding limitations, etc.

The cycle continues (without following any preconceived path) until a portfolio of ideas is collected on the major problem dimensions. The facilitator then guides the group logically toward a focal point with connects the ideas and serves as a conceptual solution (to be developed and clarified in a proposed project or design).

The Evolving Language of Innovation

Opportunity assessment

The process of perceiving, detecting and recognizing opportunities for change, new technologies, products or solutions; may not depend on detailed analysis at first but instead relies on weak signals from the external environment. Often serves as the initial stimulus for an innovation project. (See: *Weak signals*)

Paradigm shift

In the context of innovation, the term is often used (and abused) in connection with a major change in thought and personal beliefs or a radical change in complex systems or businesses.

Parking lot

During an ideation session, this is an area where the facilitator records ideas and concerns that are tangential to the current session, but which have value for another session or phase of the project.

Paraphrasing

To paraphrase is to capture the meaning or at least the basic characteristics of someone's idea or viewpoint. To contribute to a healthy climate for innovation, it is often necessary to repeat the meaning of someone's comment or idea in your own words and not simply repeat their words verbatim. (See: *Offer*)

Personalized messaging

A one-to-one communications method which relies on technology and analytics to create and deliver individualized messages and offers to consumers (or citizens).

The Evolving Language of Innovation

Persuasive communications

The process and practices used to develop messages, models and documents for a specific audience that the writer wishes to influence; relies on the knowledge and application of language, logic, evidence and information design. Documents that depend on persuasive communications include business plans, information memoranda, white papers, proposals and strategic plans.

Problem–solution structure

A logical problem-solving approach and communications pattern that relies on a sequential process. Provides details on a problem, and proceeds through analysis and conclusions to ideas and recommendations.

This structure is the opposite of lateral thinking and headlining techniques for presenting ideas. (See: *Lateral thinking*)

Process innovation

Changes and improvements in an organization's process, for example in business operations, financial management, marketing, product development, business development, human resources management.

Usually concentrates on improving efficiencies and effectiveness, but may sometimes focus on creating a new form of business model or providing a mechanism for entering new markets.

Product innovation

Development of new products or improvements in old products and services. May involve creation of a unique mix of services to complement an old product.

Introduction of the new product or service may also provide opportunities for new approaches to market entry, partnerships, promotion, distribution channels, packaging, and thought leadership.

Project sponsor

Someone who provides the initial impetus for an innovation project and team formation; takes a major role in identifying the project goals, selecting team members, coaching the facilitators, and securing funding and other resources. May provide a vision of the desired outcome. (See: *Visionary*)

Protocept

An emerging product idea or concept that is crafted and refined through experiment and simulation (prior to prototype design).

Random stimulus

Creativity methods that rely on exploratory thinking stimulated by random words, images or sounds. Groups are presented with a random stimulus and asked to explore associations that produce new ideas

Rating model

A system of criteria used to rate ideas, alternative concepts and other intangibles. Scales typically extend from 1 to 10. The rating model defines the outcome that qualifies an idea or concept for each numbered rating.

Reversal method

A provocative method of creativity requiring the idea generator to take a situation as it is currently understood and turn it around; provides a means of escaping from the old way of looking at a problem or challenge.

> "By disrupting the traditional mode of thinking, one frees information that may come together in a new way . . . by making the reversal, one moves to a new position. Then one sees what happens." De Bono, p. 143

Roadmapping

A planning process designed to support strategy and visionary thinking; relies on collaborative and graphical techniques; useful in identifying the actions, innovation and resources needed to implement a long-term vision.

S-curve

The theory that most innovations spread through a market or society in the form of an S-curve, e.g., early adopters try the innovation first (market grows slowly along the curve), followed by a majority (rapid growth), and finally leading to acceptance by the mass market (growth plateau).

This theory was first introduced by E. M. Rogers who said a customer's attitude toward a new technology or product went through five stages: Knowledge, Persuasion, Decision, Implementation and Confirmation.

Scenario planning

A planning technique that relies on using available knowledge to create plausible future situations; sometimes used in conjunction with systems thinking methods. (See: *Market framing*)

> "Scenario planning simplifies the avalanche of data into a limited number of possible states or scenarios. Each scenario tells a story of how the various elements might interact under a variety of different assumptions." – Paul J. H. Schoemaker

Screening matrix

A method of choosing a group of ideas for further development; usually a two-dimensional matrix with 'attractiveness' along one axis and 'compatibility' (or another relevant measure) along the second axis.

Self censor

A pattern of negative thinking which causes an individual to critically evaluate emerging ideas which are internally generated; resulting in the ideas being suppressed (the opposite of *exploratory thinking*). The self censor is usually more prevalent when there is a poor climate for innovation.

Segmentation analytics

Use of research and models to discover distinct groups of customers (or citizens) based on shared characteristics; used to improve communications and deliver services, solutions or apps for each targeted group.

The Evolving Language of Innovation

Shared paradigm | Shared purpose

A jointly defined model and dialogue where participants in an innovation project share a vision of success and achieve a high level of trust, knowledge sharing and cooperative energy.

Single niche strategy

A strategy to overcome a technology barrier and offer an innovative product or service that enables a firm to establish competitive leadership in a specific niche.

This is an appropriate strategy when competitors cannot deliver the innovation at a reasonable price (due to technology or other barriers). The firm that moves first to remove the barriers can dominate the niche. (MacMillan and McGrath, p. 164.)

Situational leadership

A theory of organization stating that different and flexible leadership styles and models are needed for different situations.

In an innovation project, a leader with a quality-centric style ("get it right the first time") may have to adjust his or her style to confront the risks of innovation (when people rarely get it right on the first try).

Smart specialization

A national (or regional) approach to innovation policy, where countries (or regions) focus on selected priorities—based on analysis of assets and core strengths—as a way to decide on knowledge-based projects, research, and partnerships.

The Evolving Language of Innovation

Social innovation

Creation and development of new solutions, strategies, concepts, partnerships and organizational models that meet the needs of citizens and strengthen society (e.g., in education, healthcare, urban revitalization, community improvements, etc.).

May take place in the public sector, non-profit groups, or through collaborative partnerships involving public, private, and academic entities (see *Megacommunity).*

Soft innovation

A form of innovation (usually not based on technologies) involving changes in products in *creative industries* (or changes in the aesthetic features of products in other industries).

Soft skills

A cluster of behavioral traits, personal habits and use of language that affect interaction with individuals and groups. Includes persuasive communications, creativity, strategic thinking and conflict resolution.

Springboards

A form of wishful thinking and expression used to assist in the process of idea generation. Includes "I wish" and "How to" statements and the application of images, connections, analogies and paraphrasing. (See: *Synectics*)

Storyboard method

A form of idea development that goes beyond brainstorming methods; more organized than brainstorming. Enables a group to visualize, think and collaborate on a complex challenge. The collaboration involves creation of a structured, visual picture of how a solution might be implemented.

Suspended judgment

The ability of innovators to reserve their evaluation (and judgment) of new and emerging ideas. The goal in suspended judgment is to give idea generators an opportunity to develop their ideas into more concrete concepts before subjecting them to critical analysis and decisions.

Synectics

An approach to innovation and problem-solving that stimulates new modes of thought of which the participant is generally unaware. Attempts to discover new and surprising solutions in ideation sessions by combining a structured approach to innovation with the spontaneous technique of brainstorming.

More complicated than brainstorming due to many steps, idea triggers and unique terminology; originally developed by the consulting firm Synectics, Inc., George Prince, William Gordon, and others. (See: *In/out listening, task headlines, springboards*)

Systems thinking

An approach to planning and problem solving that treats complex challenges as parts of an overall system, rather than focusing on piecemeal solutions and individual outcomes; based on a belief that parts of a system are best understood in the context of relationships with each other and with other systems.

Tacit knowledge

Information and knowledge that an individual develops over time, often as a specialized skill, ability or method; may be difficult to articulate. Usually not documented or recorded. Can sometimes be demonstrated or taught to others or transferred through observation. (See: *Codified knowledge*)

Two major types are technical tacit knowledge (e.g. "know-how") and cognitive tacit knowledge (e.g., beliefs and mental models). Many organizations capture tacit knowledge through mentoring, knowledge-sharing, specialized portals, and expert documentation (e.g. thought leadership studies).

Task headline

A carefully crafted one-sentence headline statement of what you expect a group to work on during an innovation session.

> "Unless there is articulated agreement by the group concerning what approach they are going take to the problem, there is confusion, because everyone works in his or her exclusive framework." Prince, p.26

Technology transfer

A process and system for sharing knowledge, specialized skills, technologies, software, manufacturing methods, and processes between and among corporate entities, universities, government organizations.

Sometimes used to commercially exploit research and new product concepts through licensing, joint ventures, development agreements and other partnerships designed to reduce risks and costs and share in the value generated.

> "Transfer = Transmission + Absorption
> ... if knowledge is not absorbed, it has not been transferred." Davenport and Prusak, p.101

Thought leadership

The intersection of knowledge management and marketing communications to demonstrate leadership in topics of interest to customers, partners, suppliers, other stakeholders and opinion leaders.

Threshold of acceptance

The point on an idea spectrum between acceptable and unacceptable where an idea becomes usable in the minds of decision makers. Through the *itemized response* technique, a rough idea is modified to overcome its uncertainties and risks and vault over the threshold. (See: *Synectics*)

Transformation value model

A process model to assist planners with complex problems involving how to accomplish significant changes in government and business organizations. Provides a dialogue for planners and promotes the combination of techniques from innovation management with strategic tools and objectives.

Transformational innovation

A process to create breakthrough products and solutions, and new business models. May involve disruptive change in existing markets or creation of new markets. High risk in comparison to core innovation or adjacent innovations. [Nagji and Tuff, 2012

Triple helix model

A model of university-industry-government interactions, based on theories that cooperation of these previously independent spheres is key to innovation and economic development in knowledge-based societies. The model suggests that when hybrid entities such as technology transfer departments in universities and government R&D labs interact with venture capitalists, entrepreneurs and technology-driven firms, the result is higher innovation capacity, value creation and economic growth.

Trust equation

A conceptual model to assist innovation teams in communicating and collaborating on the issues of risk-taking, knowledge sharing and role clarity.

Type I versus Type II errors

Types of errors encountered in a decision-making process. A Type I error, also known as a "false positive", occurs when you observe or perceive a difference when in actual fact there is none. A Type II error, also known as a "false negative" is an error of failing to observe a difference when in truth there is one. (Based on the work of Neyman and Pearson, 1928)

For the innovation management professional, a Type II error is an error of excessive skepticism regarding an attractive opportunity.

Value blueprint

A mapping tool (designed by Ron Adner) to "help teams locate and identify the different sources of risk that lie outside their project." Helps strategists to clarify a position in an ecosystem and discover ways to overcome barriers to innovation. [Adner, 2013]

Value creation

An activity or process that creates new assets, growth, knowledge or other objects of strategic value through learning, acquisition and technology transfer. (See: *Knowledge investment*)

Vertical thinking

An approach to decision-making and problem-solving that depends on an analytical, judgmental and usually sequential process (See: *Lateral thinking*)

Visionary

Someone who provides conceptual views and ideas on future opportunities. Usually skilled in describing future scenarios and sketching how a favorable outcome can become reality. Believes strongly in the innovation team's ability to control its process and destiny.

Vivid message

A technique used to persuade an audience or stakeholder by appealing to the imagination or making an emotional connection. Effectiveness of a vivid message is determined by the extent that it captures interest and attention and achieves the desired impact.

The Evolving Language of Innovation

Weak signals

Subtle changes and discontinuities in an industry or business environment; usually discovered in market, competitive or technology trends. Detecting weak signals often serves as the *entry point* for innovation projects and idea generation activities. (See: *Entry point*)

White space mapping

A visual tool to help groups search for, discover and articulate new opportunities, typically in underserved or unserved markets – and perhaps in markets outside the core business.
The white space is an area where products and services do not currently exist (or may exist in a form that leaves space for innovation and change).

Wicked problems

Problems that resist solution because of complex interdependencies or contradictory issues which are difficult to recognize or articulate. A wicked problem has "no definitive formulation–understanding the problem is part of the problem. Each wicked problem is unique–there are no prototypical solutions." [Erwin, 2014]

Working control

Having significant control of the direction, resources and content of an innovation project or meeting.

> "There are appropriate roles for each participant in a meeting. If these are understood and adhered to, the probability of success can be substantially increased." Prince, p. 53

"The limits of my language
means the limits of my world."
– Ludwig Wittgenstein

REFERENCES

Adler, Paul; Hecksher, Charles and Prusak, Laurence. "Building a Collaborative Enterprise," Harvard Business Review, July-August 2011

Adner, Ron. *The Wide Lens.* Penguin Group, 2013

Ansoff, Igor. "Strategies for Diversification," Harvard Business Review, Vol. 35, Sep – Oct 1957

Bettinghaus, Erwin P. and Cody, Michael J. *Persuasive Communications.* Harcourt Brace Jovanovich, 1987

Chesbrough, Henry. *Open Innovation: The New Imperative for Creating and Profiting from Technology.* Harvard Business School Press (Boston), 2003

Davenport, Thomas H. and Prusak, Laurence. *Working Knowledge.* Harvard Business School Press (Boston), 1998

Day, George S. and Schoemaker, Paul J. H. *Managing Emerging Technologies.* John Wiley & Sons, Inc, 2003

De Bono, Edward. *Lateral Thinking: Creativity Step by Step.* Harper & Row Publishers (New York), 1990

Drucker, Peter. *Innovation and Entrepreneurship*. Harper & Row (New York), 1985

Erwin, Kim. *Communicating the New*. John Wiley & Sons, Inc. (Hoboken, NJ), 2014

Etzkowitz, H., Dzisah, J., Ranga, M., and Zhou, C. *The Triple Helix Model of Innovation*. Tech Monitor, Jan-Feb 2007

Gerencser, Mark, Van Lee, R. Napolitano, F. and Kelly, C. *Megacommunities*. Palgrave Macmillan. (New York), 2008

Glasco, Jon. *Web 2.0 and Government Transformation: How E-Government and Social Media Contribute to Innovation in Public Services*. IGI Global, 2012

Glasco, Jon. *Breakthrough! Innovation Management in Practice* [Fourth edition], Aug 2017

Grove, Andrew. *Only the Paranoid Survive*. Profile Books Ltd. (London), 1998

Higgins, James M. *101 Creative Problem-Solving Techniques*. New Management Publishing Company, Inc., 1994

Kaner, Sam. *Facilitator's Guide to Participatory Decision-Making* [Second edition] Jossey-Bass (San Francisco), 2007

Katz, Bruce and Wagner, Julie. "The Rise of Innovation Districts." Brookings Institution, Metropolitan Policy Program, May 2014

Kepner, C. H. and Tregoe, B. B. *The Rational Manager.* McGraw-Hill Book Company (New York), 1965

Lindgardt, Zhenya; Reeves, Martin; Stalk, George; and Deimler, Michael S. "Business Model Innovation: When the Game Gets Tough, Change the Game." Boston Consulting Group, 2009

MacMillan, Ian C. and McGrath, Rita G. *Technology Strategy in Lumpy Market Landscapes.* (in *Managing Emerging Technologies,* Day and Schoemaker. John Wiley & Sons, Inc.), 2003

Moore, James F. *The Death of Competition: Leadership and Strategy in the Age of Business Ecosystems.* Harper Business (New York), 1996

Nagji, Bansi and Tuff, Geoff. "Managing Your Innovation Portfolio." Harvard Business Review, May 2012

Nolan, Vincent. *The Innovator's Handbook.* Sphere Books Ltd., Penguin Group (London), 1987

Osterwalder, A.; Yves Pigneur, Yves; Smith, Alan; and 470 practitioners from 45 countries. *Business Model Generation,* (self published), 2010

Prahalad, C. K. and Ramaswamy, Venkat. *The Future of Competition: Co-Creating Unique Value With Customers.* Harvard Business Review Press, 2004

Prince, George. *The Practice of Creativity.* Collier Books (New York), 1970

Rogers, Everett M. *Diffusion of Innovation* [Fourth edition]. The Free Press (New York), 1995

Sullivan, Patrick H. *Profiting from Intellectual Capital.* John Wiley & Sons, Inc. (New York), 1998.

Thomke, Stefan. *Enlightened Experimentation, The New Imperative for Innovation.* HBR on Innovation | Harvard Business School Press (Boston), 2001

Wikipedia, the Free Encyclopedia; Wikipedia Foundation, Inc. (San Francisco)

ABOUT THE AUTHOR

Jon Glasco is a freelance writer and consultant with an international background in business communications, technical writing and innovation management services.

Since the early 1990s, he delivers services to clients in Europe and North America.

Jon provides communications, innovation and process design services to help clients develop and clarify innovation strategies; communicate with stakeholders; and write business plans, strategy documents, information memoranda, thought leadership content, and technical publications.

He serves clients in smart city planning, smart mobility, urban innovation, telecommunications, public transport, fire safety, and professional services.

His clients have included AirTouch International (San Francisco), Alstom Transport (New York), Chevron Shipping (San Francisco), Electronic Data Systems (Dallas), A T. Kearney (Chicago), Ernst & Young (San Francisco), ONE GmbH (Vienna), Transport Systems Catapult (Milton Keynes), and UTC Fire and Security (Barcelona).

Jon holds an MBA and Bachelor of Science in Electrical Engineering.

www.linkedin.com/in/jonglasco/

Twitter: @jonglasco

Recommended reading

Breakthrough!
Innovation Management in Practice

How to overcome barriers to innovation
and transform ideas and models
into new products, services
and solutions

Jon Glasco

. . . based on 25+ years in research, analysis and experience in projects and companies worldwide, this edition is an **essential handbook for transforming ideas and concepts into new technologies, products, services and new-to-the-world solutions.**

. . 154 pages with informative graphics and tables that deliver a unique perspective and practical guidelines on how to manage the strategy and process of innovation, create a healthy climate for innovators, and ensure quality of communications.

Available from online booksellers:
Paperback (ISBN-10: 1452830800)